How tahajjud saved my life.

First published by SJ Writes 2023

Copyright © 2023 by Saba Jaleel

All rights reserved. No part of this publication may be reproduced, stored or transmitted in any form or by any means, electronic, mechanical, photocopying, recording, scanning, or otherwise without written permission from the publisher. It is illegal to copy this book, post it to a website, or distribute it by any other means without permission.

Saba Jaleel asserts the moral right to be identified as the author of this work.

Saba Jaleel has no responsibility for the persistence or accuracy of URLs for external or third-party Internet Websites referred to in this publication and does not guarantee that any content on such Websites is, or will remain, accurate or appropriate.

Designations used by companies to distinguish their products are often claimed as trademarks. All brand names and product names used in this book and on its cover are trade names, service marks, trademarks and registered trademarks of their respective owners. The publishers and the book are not associated with any product or vendor mentioned in this book. None of the companies referenced within the book have endorsed the book.

First edition

ISBN: 978-1-3999-7503-2

*This book was professionally typeset on Reedsy.
Find out more at reedsy.com*

I dedicate this book to all of my TikTok followers who have encouraged, supported, and rooted for my healing journey this year.

Bismillah -ir-Rahman-ir-Rahim, in the name of Allah (God), The Merciful, The Compassionate.

The night is long, and your Lord is generous.

~Unknown

Contents

Acknowledgement	iii
Why and when I knew I needed to pray tahajjud	1
So what is tahajjud?	8
The first time I prayed tahajjud	13
How to pray tahajjud	18
What difference did tahajjud make to my every day life?	26
Do I still pray tahajjud?	34
Were my du'aas really answered?	39
Tahajjud Testimonies	47
Testimony One	48
Testimony Two	51
Testimony Three	52
Testimony Four	53
Testimony Five	55
Testimony Six	56
Testimony Seven	58
Testimony Eight	59
Testimony Nine	60
Testimony Ten	61
Testimony Eleven	62
Testimony Twelve	64
Testimony Thirteen	66
Testimony Fourteen	67

Testimony Fifteen	68
Testimony Sixteen	70
Testimony Seventeen	72
Testimony Eighteen	74
Testimony Nineteen	75
Testimony Twenty	77
Testimony Twenty-One	78
Testimony Twenty-Two	79
Testimony Twenty-Three	80
Testimony Twenty-Four	81
Testimony Twenty-Five	82
Testimony Twenty-Six	83
Testimony Twenty-Seven	84
Testimony Twenty-Eight	86
Testimony Twenty-Nine	87
Testimony Thirty	89
Testimony Thirty-One	90
Testimony Thirty-Two	92
Testimony Thirty-Three	94
Testimony Thirty-Four	96
Testimony Thirty-Five	97
Testimony Thirty-Six	98
Testimony Thirty-Seven	99
Testimony Thirty-Eight	100
Testimony Thirty-Nine	101
Testimony Forty	102
Afterword	104
About the Author	107

Acknowledgement

Special thanks to Nafisa (Nick) and Annis who have been by my side through thick and thin. Two sisters who have played the roles of a mother, soul-sister, and confidant.

Thank you to Shameema, Mehraj, and Jayde. My cherished childhood best friends who have supported all of my endeavours, and always remind me of who I am.

A heartfelt thanks to Esi who saw some of my darkest days this year. A loving colleague and dear friend.

Thank you to my father who has respected the time and space I have needed alone in order to complete this book.

Thank you to my sisters Samera and Merium who despite their busy lives in motherhood, still find the time to listen to my crazy ideas and encourage all of my ambitions for the future.

Thank you to my cousin Teseen and my brother-in-law Moheeb. Without the conception and birth of my niece Aiza-Parveen, I may have never learned of what tahajjud was.

Warmest thanks to my ocean eyes. The person who cast light into my heart once again without even realising.

Lastly, thank you to all those who have broken me for you have led me back to my Rab. You are sincerely and whole-heartedly forgiven.

Why and when I knew I needed to pray tahajjud

In the last six months of 2022, I went through what I could only now describe as the most mentally challenging time of my life thus far. I have been through a lot throughout the twenty-nine years of my life here, however I had never felt as disconnected from everything and everyone around me then I had then.

It felt as though every hardship I had ever endured was stringing together to create a breakdown. I was in a place of crisis, deep emptiness, and confusion. I started to see the dunya (*world*) differently. I started hating it to the point I decided I didn't want it anymore. Not permanently, but I just wanted everything to stop for a little while. I longed for an empty space to release my darkest thoughts into an entity that could absorb it all into nothing. I wished to scream every single emotion of anger, fear, and trauma into a vessel I could close forever. I truly felt I could see no way out. The dunya was swallowing me whole with shaitan *(satan)* just watching, reaping up his success.

Suicidal thoughts became normal; as did hating myself. I blamed my unhappiness on me. I started to collect more and more anger toward myself, until I could no longer stand to look at my own reflection. When I did…it was a horrible experience. I judged every part of what I could see, and would not step away from the mirror until I was satisfied with spewing hatred at myself. I then felt relieved that I had punished the person that was living this bitter, hollow life.

Minutes turned into days, and days turned into weeks of feeling that way. I was fed up of everything negatively consuming me, and I was forever loathing in self-pity. I was aware of my traumas, but had never really faced them; truly face them for everything they had possessed me with. I felt suffocated by grief and loneliness. I cried myself to sleep, too many times. I watched the sunrise without a wink of sleep, too many times. But what I was most fed up with, was waking up with the disappointment of Allah allowing me to spend another day in what felt like an inescapable mental prison.

The frustration and stress began showing itself in my every day life. I had no interest in feeding myself, I had no care in how I was presenting at work. I had no energy to give my friends and family, and I had no shame in neglecting my faith. I realised I was wasting so much time feeling sad, that I had no strength to even attempt to pave a way out of that darkness.

The outlets I was choosing to 'help', merely just covered the

Why and when I knew I needed to pray tahajjud

reality of what was really happening. The unhealthy coping strategies became a blanket of comfort, though it struggled to warm the cold that had found its home in my soul. My heart felt dead, as did my mind. I felt I had no control over my body and my actions and that one day soon, I would make a mistake that would cost me my life. At the time I didn't care. In fact, I was waiting for Allah to present me with a way out; whether it was a sickness or a freak accident.

Looking back, I recognise the issues that were escalating this all. It was a cultivation of people letting me down, one after the other. Past traumas bouncing their weight over my shoulders 24/7. Lack of emaan *(belief)* in that Allah would help me. Little progress in securing a future companion. No real growth in my personal goals or work career. Reduced fulfilment in things that used to once make me happy, and decreased satisfaction in the time I was spending with anybody. Every moment felt like it was rotting my body to the core. I felt it was just a matter of time before it dissolved my life into its final stages.

So what could I do? Where would I start? How would I try to fix this mess?

To be honest, I always knew. I allowed waswasa *(devil whispers)* to consume my mind in every way you could imagine possible. The tests and obstacles presented themselves in my path, and I would ignorantly welcome them with open arms. The poison of delving into things that were useless and sinful, became easy to indulge in.

Ultimately, I just was not at peace. I started to heavily isolate.

Only this time it was a positive period of isolation. I started talking to Allah as if He were right next to me. After I had a bad day, I would slump myself onto the edge of my bed and pour my heart out to Him. I would tell Allah I was angry, tired, lonely. I would sob helplessly whilst staring blankly out of my bedroom windows. I was waiting patiently to feel comfort and love from Him and I was, but I could feel it wasn't enough and I had only just scratched the surface of true healing.

Weeks went by, and I now started to enjoy my conversations with Allah (SWT) *(Subhanahu Wa Ta'ala/Glorified and Exalted)*. I would not only talk to Him when I was angry or sad, but also when I was happy and content. I looked forward to going home to an empty house. Something I had once had a deep fear of. I was glad to be in conversation with my Rab *(Lord)*. It was me against the world just like it always had been, but this time with Allah by my side.

When I started to feel fulfilment from my conversations with Allah, the waswasa from shaitan weakened significantly. I paid more attention to pleasing Allah than pleasing the easy, temporary ways out. I removed the monthly routine of having my nails done with ease. I placed full trust in Allah that He would replace the satisfaction I would get from it, with something better and actually beneficial for my akhirah *(afterlife)*. I reduced the amount of pointless time I wasted watching TV or Netflix. I tried to cutting out listening to music as often as I did, and I became more wary of what I was using the hours in my day doing.

I replaced my old enjoyments with spending time with animals

Why and when I knew I needed to pray tahajjud

and going for walks. Nourishing my body with a better diet and reading self-help books. Most importantly above all, I started to visit my mum at the cemetery on a weekly basis. Not only just to talk to her and make du'aas *(supplications)* at her graveside, but it was a reminder of how short life really is, and where our final destination truly lies. All healthy outlets and coping mechanisms, yet it still wasn't enough.

My family and friends would continuously remind me of salah *(prayer)* and why we **need** it. Not only was I fully aware that salah was compulsory of course, but I would often think about when I **was** praying consistently, and how I felt during that time. I worked tirelessly internally to remind myself of how worship had once made me feel. Once upon a time, years ago, I observed both hijab (head-covering) and niqab (face veil). I had been out of work for nearly one whole year. I dedicated all my time in researching into the crevices of Islam and the sole beauty of it. I had encompassed all of this wealthy knowledge, and yet I was ignorant in how it could save me from my darkest traumas and life stresses.

Beginning of 2023 was when the huge leaps I had made toward my healing journey in 2022, truly started to unravel. I had been journaling after heavy reflection periods because I knew one day soon…I would feel better.

I started to pray salah again. I would attempt to wake up for fajr *(morning prayer)* with little success, however I did not let it stop me from praying the rest of the five daily prayers. I was determined to feel at peace again, and I knew there was only one way to do this. That was simply to obey Allah, and do what my body was beautifully created to do; and that was worship my Lord.

I started to feel alive again, and now that I had tasted that tiny piece of satisfaction, I wanted more. I wanted Allah to save me. Not a GP, not a therapist, not pharmaceutical drugs. I wanted my Rab to embrace me in His mercy and hold me until I breathed my last breath.

One night in conversation with Allah, I remembered a story. My cousin and her husband struggled for two years to conceive a child. Even after so many different methods advised by GP and other health professionals, they were not successful in conceiving. They both, together, prayed a special prayer for several weeks and by the will of Allah within this time, my cousin found out she was pregnant with their first child. My brother-in-law had also prayed this same night prayer for my cousin to have a quick, painless, and simple birth. My cousin told me they would pray this particular prayer in the middle of the night, and often. I remembered what the prayer was called, and I also remembered recalling my cousins birth. She, Alhamdulilah *(praise be to God)*, had a relatively quick, healthy, and successful birth. I believed this to be solely the result of…tahajjud.

One night, I obsessed with the research on the tahajjud prayer. I was expecting it to be a prayer that was difficult to observe. One that you would have to learn to recite separate surahs *(Quranic chapters)* or du'aas for. I was wrong. When I had stumbled upon how pure and simple tahajjud was, I knew then that this was it.

Why and when I knew I needed to pray tahajjud

Tahajjud was what was going to save my life.

So what is tahajjud?

Whilst I could sit here and type many different explanations of what tahajjud is, I have every intention of describing tahajjud in this chapter as simply as possible. This is for the mere fact that Islam comes with little complication because it is in fact a religion of peace, purity, and perfection, and needn't any confusion or complex adaptations.

Tahajjud is a voluntary prayer that is specifically offered in the night. Tahajjud itself, is an Arabic word that is derived from '*hajada*'. 'One, he slept or slept in the night or in the latter part of the night; two, he remained awake or was sleepless or wakeful in the night; three he awoke from sleep to pray or for some other purpose; four he prayed in the night.' Many also align tahajjud salat *(prayer)* with Qiyam al-Layl *(standing at night/standing performing prayers).* I had always noticed this time in my prayer apps, but had no idea what it actually referred to.

So what is tahajjud?

And he said: "You should pray Qiyaam al-Layl, for it is the custom of the righteous who came before you and it brings you closer to your Lord, and expiates sins and prevents misdeeds." [Narrated by al-Tirmidhi]

There is a difference of opinion amongst scholars as to whether Qiyaam al-Layl and tahajjud are one of the same, but what we do know is waking **from** your sleep to voluntary offer nafl (*voluntary*) prayers, is indeed more compelling and rewarding.

Shaykhul Hadith, Moulana Zakariyya Kandehlawi (rahimahullah) says: "Tahajjud refers to the salah one offers after awakening from a sleep. Offering nafl salah after isha with the intention of salatul layl will also constitute tahajjud in the metaphorical sense." [Taqrir Bukhari, part 4, pg.24]

Both prayers would be considered as tahajjud in sha Allah (*God willing*).

* * *

Growing up, I was made aware of the different kinds of prayers by my mother. I was taught about fard (*compulsory*), sunnah (*encouraged*), and nafl (*voluntary*) salah, though I was never aware of any specific prayer made in the middle of the night.

I would always however, recall the beauty of when my sisters and I would stay awake as young teenagers every Ramadaan, solely in the hope that we would be praying on Laylut-al-Qadr (*Night of Power*). I recall the feeling of immense power and love I would feel when staying up all night praying two rak'ahs *(unit of prayers)*, upon two rak'ahs, upon several, until we could no longer stand. I recall, regardless of how fatigue we became, how weak our legs would feel and how sleep deprived we were, the next day we would always awake feeling renewed and so spiritually cleansed. It is only now as an adult I have understood why we may have felt these emotions.

The Lord descends every night to the lowest heaven when one-third of the night remains and says: "Who will call upon Me, that I may answer him? Who will ask of Me, that I may give him? Who will seek My forgiveness that I may forgive him?" [Al-Bukhari, Sahih Muslim]

Our Rab has told us that He is closest to us during the last third of the night.

Our Rab has told us in the Holy Qur'aan that worshipping Him in the midst of the night, will also raise us in status.

"And from [part of] the night, pray with it as additional [worship] for you; it is expected that your Lord will resurrect you to a praised station." Qur'aan, Surah Al-Isra {17:79}

Tahajjud is a prayer bursting full of infinite love and mercy.

Tahajjud is a prayer that helps you attain a unique closeness with your Rab.

So what is tahajjud?

Tahajjud is a prayer that is voluntary yet so powerful in its might.

Tahajjud is a prayer that unties our knotted minds with clarity and ease.

Tahajjud is a prayer that Allah (AWJ) (*Azzawajjal/Mighty and Dominant*) has promised its outcome will always be success.

Tahajjud is a prayer that heals sorrows and your inner most deepest wounds.

Tahajjud is a prayer that fulfils your desires and waters the emptiness within your soul.

Tahajjud is a prayer that washes away your sins and shields you with a radiant nur *(light)*.

Tahajjud is prayer that graces you with endurance for this dunya with patience and faith.

Tahajjud is prayer that will open doors that you could never imagine possible.

Tahajjud is a prayer that cannot be described with words but is felt with the 'qalb' *(heart)*.

Tahajjud is prayer that will follow to bring countless blessings into your life spiritually, emotionally, and physically.

"The du'aa made at tahajjud is like an arrow that doesn't miss it's

target." [Imam Ash Shafi'i]

The first time I prayed tahajjud

At the beginning of my tahajjud journey, I had chosen to document it through recording a video every morning with updates. I knew I wasn't the only one struggling. I had the intention of sharing this one day, but also use it as driving force in holding myself accountable in it becoming a success.

I first set my alarm for 4am along with my fajr alarm, with zero expectations of what would even happen.

As expected, my alarm went off *(on a school night by the way)* and it had felt like I had just completed ten rounds in the ring with Mike Tyson. It was cold in my room, I felt like I was on a completely different planet, and I knew I had very little energy in physically attempting to get out of my bed and make wudhu *(ablution)*.

I failed first time, yes.

How tahajjud saved my life.

Did I give up?

Absolutely not.

I did the same the following night. I set my alarm for the same time, made the same intention, and proceeded to fall asleep after reciting my usual adkhars *(remembrance/protective prayers; **please do not forget to pray these!**)*

Again, I remember snoozing the alarm several times before I eventually cancelled it completely.

I woke up feeling immense guilt and shame.

Did I give up?

Absolutely not.

In the days that followed for nearly two weeks, this became a repetitive and exhausting cycle.

I would set my alarm every day, but failed to physically get out from the 'comfort' of my bed.

My mental health was still rapidly declining, but my trust in Allah remained firm. I knew He would make this easy for me had I continued to pursue this goal, and persevere through all the waswasa and hardship I was facing.

I started noticing two weeks in that my body clock was changing. As I had been in a steady routine of waking up at this

The first time I prayed tahajjud

particular time for a number of days, I was feeling less distressed when the alarm would go off. My body was adjusting, and almost expecting to wake up at 4am. This gave me a glimmer of hope.

Third week of trying to wake up for tahajjud, I started becoming disheartened. I really wanted to wake up with ease. I wanted Allah to call me to Him. I wanted to wake up naturally without an alarm, but it wasn't at that point working out for me.

I knew that tahajjud salah is most recommended and beneficial in the last third of the night, but I also knew tahajjud is also accepted after isha *(night prayer)* or before fajr.

Hasan Basri (rahimahullah) said: "One who offers salah after isha has prayed tahajjud." [Tafsir Tabari, Surah Isra, Ayah: 79]

Although this wasn't what I intended, I knew I had to start somewhere. I prayed tahajjud a handful of times after isha. Whilst it still felt rewarding and special, I was still disappointed with not being able to wake up in the night. None the less, I had full faith that Al-Wahhab *[The Giver of Gifts]* would fulfil my desire in the most beautiful way, and at the right time.

It was narrated that Abu Darda' conveyed that the Prophet ﷺ (peace be upon him) said:"Whoever goes to bed intending to wake up and pray during the night, but is overwhelmed by sleep until morning comes, what he intended will be recorded for him, and his sleep is a charity given to him by his Lord." [Sunan Ibn Majah, 1344]

How tahajjud saved my life.

* * *

I remember the day so clearly.

I had my hijama *(cupping therapy)* done on Jummuah *(Friday)*, 10th March. Before my hijama therapist started my session, I made sincere du'aas. I asked Allah to weaken all of my afflictions, and break down any barriers and obstacles that were preventing me from rebuilding my relationship with Him.

After my session as usual, I was feeling refreshed yet drained, and also ready to just go home and pray tahajjud. When I had gotten home, I knew that I was absolutely shattered from the working week, and with having my hijama done on top, I was convinced that there was no way I was realistically going to wake up at 4am for tahajjud. So I made wudhu and solely prayed isha. In the last sujood *(prostration)* of that isha salah, I was specific and heartfelt in my du'aas regarding tahajjud.

I prayed my adkhars, still set my alarm as usual for a slightly later time of 4:30am, and then went to sleep.

I recall waking and opening my eyes like I had already slept. I felt an overwhelming wave of tranquillity and was smiling to myself from cheek to cheek *(I like to think the angels too were smiling with me!)*. I hurried to find my phone so I could check the time. 4:10am. I was in complete disbelief. Not only was I feeling so so happy beyond explanation, Allah had woken me up **before** my alarm. I hurried to turn my preset alarm off, and

The first time I prayed tahajjud

opened Snapchat to record that very moment.

That moment has now become a core memory of mine.

I could hear the birds tweeting away, the moon was shining so brightly through my windows, and I was feeling mind-numbingly euphoric.

I made wudhu, prayed four rak'ahs, and then cried to Allah. I poured the contents of my weary heart and soul to Al-Wadud [*The Loving One*], and sat for an hour in the presence of Al-Quddus [*The Most Sacred*].

I then sat on the comfort of my prayer mat doing dhikr (*remembrance of God*), whilst I patiently waited for fajr time.

Allah reassured them, "Have no fear! I am with you, hearing and seeing." Qur'aan, Surah Ta-ha {20:46}

I woke up in the morning feeling like I was on cloud nine. I could not stop smiling. I was in awe of my Rab's mercy, and I felt a huge sense of accomplishment. My heart was still broken, but it felt rested.

Abd Allah ibn Salam (may Allah be pleased with him) reports that the Messenger of Allah ﷺ (peace be upon him) said, "O people! Spread the salams, feed others, maintain family ties, and pray at night when others sleep and you will enter Heaven safely." [Al-Tirmidhi, Hakim]

So now you are wondering how one should pray tahajjud right?

How to pray tahajjud

Tahajjud is not a complicated prayer and I **must** stress this. Although praying tahajjud is straight forward in how it has been prescribed, what many of us including myself experience as the main struggle, is to actually wake up for it. I have spoken to several Muslims this year that have shared their difficulties in being able to wake up for tahajjud. I can heavily relate to this as initially, it was most definitely challenging and frustrating when it wasn't 'working' for me. I always knew that it wasn't going to be easy, but my intention remained strong.

This is key.

Intention is widely spoken about in Islam. Niyyah *(intention)* is such an important principle that plays a pivotal role in every act of worship we perform. The beauty of making niyyah is what differentiates the acts we carry out **for** Allah (SWT), to those of little relevance, or merely done for the sake of others.

The purer and sincere your niyyah is, the bigger the reward and blessings in sha Allah.

Niyyah establishes a clear starting line for the path you seek to follow. The most beautiful part? You needn't say your intention out loud, you needn't plan it or follow any specific structure, you simply make niyyah from your heart.

The Messenger ﷺ (peace be upon him) of Allah (SWT) said, "The reward of deeds depends upon the intention and every person will get the reward according to what he has intended. So whoever emigrated for Allah and His Apostle, then his emigration was for Allah and His Apostle. And whoever emigrated for worldly benefits or for a woman to marry, his emigration was for what he emigrated for." [Sahih Bukhari, Kitab-ul-Imaan, Hadith No. 53]

I started with first calculating when the last third of the night starts. I did this very easily using the following website: https://thirdofthenight.com

You enter the time of fajr where you reside, paired with the time of maghreb *(sunset prayer)* where you reside. The time stated in the result, will then reflect when the most ideal time for praying tahajjud *begins.*

The last third of the night is said to run from this time, right up until 20-30 minutes before fajr salah. This means there is ample time to pray it.

Once you have woken up, it is important to take your time and make wudhu. Do not rush. Enjoy the whole process from the very beginning, right up until the end.

Imam Muslim (rahimahullah) has recorded this Hadith. Sayyiduna 'Uthman ibn 'Affan (May Allah be pleased with him) reports that Rasulullah ﷺ (peace be upon him) said: "Whomsoever makes wudhu, and makes wudhu well, his (minor) sins leave his body even coming out from under his nails." [Sahih Muslim, Hadith: 245]

After making wudhu and you are dressed appropriately for salah, make your intention, but do not put pressure on yourself for this part for Allah is Al-Alim [*The All-Knowing One*].

"He knows well what lies in the hearts." Qur'aan, Surah Al-Mulk {67:13}

You can pray anywhere between 2-12 rak'ahs. After you have completed the desired amount of rak'ahs, you simply make du'aa. Hands raised, or with no hands raised. **This does not matter.**

You'll make du'aa. You'll talk to Allah. You'll cry to Allah. You'll laugh with Allah.

All the while do you know what is happening?

You are falling in love.

Tahajjud is prayer of love, a prayer of peace. In this time of solitude, you are completed isolated from the dunya, and it is just you and Al-Khaliq *[The Creator]*. You'll be surrounded by His forgiveness, comforted by His promise, and cradled by His everlasting love.

"Glorify Him at night and at the fading of the stars." Qur'aan, Surah Tur {52:49}

I truly believe there is no right or wrong in making du'aa at tahajjud time. Allah already knows what you desire, and what you are going to supplicate before you have even moved your lips.

Make your du'aa stronger with reciting extra surahs and supplications should you wish to, however remember this is optional. The conversation between you and your Lord doesn't need to be perfect. It already is perfect.

Finish with plenty of dhikr should you wish to. All that there is left to do is reap the rewards from tahajjud, and I promise the peace you feel, will override the pressure of you craving those tahajjud du'aas even being answered.

You will forget everything from this temporary life in these moments.

"The true servants of the Most Compassionate are those who walk on the earth humbly, and when the foolish address them improperly, they only respond with peace. They are those who spend a good portion of the night, prostrating themselves and standing before their Lord." Qur'aan, Surah Al-Furqan {25:63-64}

How tahajjud saved my life.

* * *

As I had become attached to tahajjud not long before Ramadaan began this year, I was not prepared for when I would not be able to pray tahajjud due to my menstrual cycle.

I cried for hours as I was just so upset that I could not pray any salah, but especially tahajjud during this time. However, after plenty of research, I was happy to learn that women can still wake up during the window of tahajjud, and still practise methods of ibadah *(worship)*.

It is still permissible to wake up for tahajjud and make du'aa without praying salah, and still have your du'aas answered. You can still sit and read Qur'aan *(without touching the Mus-haf)*, you can still make lots of dhikr of Allah, and you can still sincerely make du'aa. It is not forbidden, frowned upon, or discouraged.

So every night without fail then, and till present, I set my alarm at the chosen time. I sit up awake in my bed, make du'aa and do dhikr, and then go back to sleep.

Alhamdulilah, I have still had du'aas granted this way *(whilst not being able to pray)*.

Allahu Akbar *(Allah is Greatest)*.

So my sisters, do not feel sad when your monthly cycle comes around as you can still wake up for tahajjud with the intention of remembering, and talking with your Rab.

How to pray tahajjud

Tahajjud is your pathway to Allah. Tahajjud keeps you connected with Allah…Always.

Falling into a healthy routine of regular tahajjud, is truly the beginning of miracles unfolding before you.

Your Rab is going to answer your du'aas, for His promise is true.

"O you who have believed, seek help through patience and prayer, Indeed, Allah is with the patient." Qur'aan, Surah Al-Baqarah {2:153}

* * *

To conclude:

1. Make wudhu once you have woken up.
2. Clear your prayer space from all distractions.
3. Ensure you are dressed appropriately.
4. Make your sincere intention - what do you wish to gain from this salah?
5. Pray 2-12 rak'ahs.
6. Take your time when talking to Allah and making du'aa for whatever your heart may be seeking.
7. Use your fingers or tasbih *(prayer beads)* for some dhikr to finish.

It was narrated that Abu Hurairah said: The Messenger of Allah ﷺ (peace be upon him) said: "When any one of you goes to sleep, the shaitan ties three knots on his head, saying each time: (sleep) a long night. If he wakes up and remembers Allah (SWT), one knot is undone. If he performs wudhu, another knot is undone. If he prays, all the knots are undone and he starts his day in a good mood and feeling energetic. Otherwise he starts his day in a bad mood and feeling lethargic." [Sunan An Nasai, 1608]

Below is a list of tips/advice for tahajjud that has aided me:

1. Make du'aa after isha salah for Allah to make it easy for you to wake up.
2. Read all of your adkhars before bed and listen to Surah Al-Mulk.
3. Get into bed early so that you gain at least 5-6 hours of sleep before your alarm is set for tahajjud.
4. Keep your mobile a little far from you so it takes extra effort to turn it off.
5. Once up, remind yourself of why you wanted to wake up for tahajjud.
6. Be proud that you are following a Sunnah of the Messenger of Allah ﷺ *(peace be upon him),* and that the rewards will surely satisfy you.
7. If you are feeling extremely sleepy, drink water *(keep a bottle next to you before you sleep)* - recite a'oodhu billahi min ash-shaitan-ir-rajeem and spit on your left shoulder three times.
8. Make the most of making du'aa whilst in sujood during tahajjud - there is no rush, **especially** at that time.
9. Do lots of dhikr before and after tahajjud du'aa.

How to pray tahajjud

10. Incorporate Al-Fatiha, Ayatul Qursi, Durood-E-Ebraheem, and the four Qul before *(preferably)* tahajjud du'aa.
11. Stay awake until fajr if possible - read or listen to some Qur'aan during this time.
12. Do not neglect fajr or any of the other five daily salah as they are **fard,** and tahajjud is voluntary.

My only question now is, what is actually stopping you?

I stand firm on you do not want something badly enough, if you haven't woken up to pray tahajjud for it.

"If you want something in your life and you aren't praying Tahajjud for it then in reality you don't really want it." [Sheikh Yasir Qadhi]

What difference did tahajjud make to my every day life?

Whilst a majority of individuals want to pray tahajjud to have a specific du'aa answered, I didn't. My sole intention at the time was to gain closeness to Allah, improve my mental health, and to reduce the heaviness of the stresses I was experiencing.

My mental state was so fragile at that point, that I was afraid I would one day wake up without having the ability to see the day through. Every morning felt gut-wrenchingly empty and bleak.

As I mentioned in chapter one, I no longer wanted to stay stuck in a bitter cycle that saw me develop countless toxic ways of staying afloat. I knew I had to break this pattern…before it would completely break me.

What difference did tahajjud make to my every day life?

After praying tahajjud once, it became an addiction. We often associate this word with sinful things, but I am changing this narrative. How wonderful for me to be able to sit here after all of the challenges I have faced, and proudly say that tahajjud has become my coping mechanism. Talking with Al-Muqit *[The Nourisher]* has been absorbing my pain. Crying to An-Nur *[The Light]* has brought endless radiance into the darkest spaces of my mind. Relying on Al-Qawiyy *[The Strong One]* has given me strength to fight through my hardest battles. Trusting in Al-Wakeel *[The Trustee]* has revived my emaan in its entirety.

This year, tahajjud became my life line. I would wake up for it as if my life depended on it. And it did. If there was ever a night I woke up late or too close to fajr, I would break down in tears and felt so upset. I would ask Allah to forgive me for over sleeping, and to still accept my tahajjud prayer.

Without fail, Al Mughni *[The Enricher]* would fill me with such a serene burst of peace throughout the following day, that all my sadness and worries seemed to just melt away. My face would beam with the pride I was feeling on the inside. My mindset was growing with positivity, and I had every hope that Allah would keep this going for me…so long as I kept waking up for tahajjud.

So that is exactly what I did.

Weeks on end, right into Ramadaan 2023, I would wake up every, single, night. I would look forward to going to sleep, just because I was so excited to wake up to speak to my Lord. Beautiful no?

Tahajjud is magic in itself; but tahajjud prayed during Ramadaan? No words I could ever type would be enough to describe the vast emotion it carries.

Abdullah ibn Salam (may Allah be pleased with him) narrated, "when the Prophet ﷺ (peace be upon him) arrived for the first time in Madinah, I went with everyone to see him. When I saw him, I knew his face was not that of a liar. The first words he said were", "O people, spread Salam (greeting of peace), give food, maintain kin relationships, and pray at night while people are asleep. With this, you shall enter Heaven in peace." [Sunan Ibn Majah, 3251]

Every tahajjud, throughout each and every ruku *(bowing)* and sujood, I felt as though my heart was bursting with the love of Allah.

I no longer felt alone. I could feel Al Qareeb [*The Near One*].

"Indeed, it is we who created humankind and fully know what their souls whisper to them, and We are closer to them than their jugular vein." Qur'aan, Surah Qaf {50:16}

I found deep solace in these moments and completely detached from the dunya.

The world was silent. The world was sleeping. The world was standing still.

Day by day, night by night, I could almost feel Al Jabbar *[The Restorer]* repairing my heart; piece by piece, gently placing them all back together as if they had never been broken apart.

What difference did tahajjud make to my every day life?

The loneliness that had embedded itself into the weariness of my bones was still there undoubtedly, but it felt as though Al-Muhaymin *[The Preserver of Safety],* was clothing me with His mercy and I had a new lease for life.

You see the world so differently when you keep Al Hadi *[The Guide]* right by your side.

You begin to feel inferior, content, but most of all…*loved.*

Allah is Al-Baseer *[The All-Seeing].* He may not be before your eyes, but He is Al-Waasi *[The All-Encompassing].*

According to a Hadith narrated by Abu Hurairah, Jibreel (peace be upon him) asked the Prophet ﷺ (peace be upon him) about ihsaan. He said: "It is to worship Allah as if you can see Him, for although you cannot see Him, He can see you." [Al-Buhkari and Muslim.]

* * *

I would always begin my day with dhikr of Allah.

I tuned out the anxieties before they had a chance to cloud my day.

I strived to see the good in everybody, even those that had upset me or let me down.

Life became easier to endure.

I was grounded, humbled.

My tahajjud du'aas were slowly but surely unfolding before my eyes.

I would cry relentlessly from joy not being able to even comprehend what was actually happening.

I would stop wherever I was at the time, close my eyes and would whisper 'Alhamdulilah'.

There were many times where I felt too lucky. It was hard to fathom that a slave who had sinned over and over again, had been allowed to taste the fruits of Allah's generosity.

Remember, Allah is Al-Afuww *[The Pardoner]*. Allah is Ar-Rauf *[The Most Kind]*. Allah is Al-Ghafur *[The Great Forgiver]*.

Allah is what you think of Him, and if you think of Him as the One who is going to give you everything, He is going to give you everything.

On the authority of Abu Hurayrah (may Allah be pleased with him), who said that the Prophet ﷺ (peace be upon him) said: "Allah the Almighty said: I am as My servant thinks I am. I am with him when he makes mention of Me. If he makes mention of Me to himself, I make mention of him to Myself; and if he makes mention of Me in an assembly, I make mention of him in an assembly better than it. And if he draws near to Me an arm's length, I draw near to him a cubit,

What difference did tahajjud make to my every day life?

and if he draws near to Me a cubit, I draw near to him a fathom. And if he comes to Me walking, I go to him at speed." [Al-Buhkari, Muslim, at-Tirmidhi, and Ibn-Majah, Hadith 15, 40 Hadith Qudsi]

Tahajjud became a means of survival for me.

Without it, my days were incomplete and held no purpose.

Without it, I felt deflated and stripped of any aspirations for the future.

With it, I had more motivation to be a better Muslim and stress less.

With it, I understood that this dunya will never amount to the endless bounties of Jannah *(heaven)*.

It is easy it get lost in the temptations of this life. It is easy to allow people to break your heart. It is easy to bow down to waswasa. It is easy to crave materialistic things.

But do you know what is also easy?

It is easy to make wudhu. It is easy to sacrifice wordly goods for the sake of Allah if your intentions are pure. It is easy to forgive people who have wronged you. It is easy to find a few minutes to pray your fard salah. It is easy to open one page of the Qur'aan and read it. It is easy to give your heart to Allah and trust Him with it. It is easy to replace sin with deeds when you are desperate for His rewards.

How tahajjud saved my life.

All of this is dependant on your love for Islam and Allah. I am confident in guaranteeing that making tahajjud a part of your regular routine, will provide you with an unbreakable foundation of power and hope.

* * *

Below is a list of tips/advice that has helped me stay consistent in growing my inner peace, attaining self-worth, and building my bond with Al-Waali *[The Protecting Friend]***:**

1. Try your utmost best in reducing major and minor sins.
2. Reduce the amount of time spent watching TV, listening to music, hours spent on social media *(if unproductive)*.
3. Talk to Allah throughout the day - remember Him in everything you do; saying Bismillah (in the name of God), Alhamdulilah, SubhanAllah *(Glory be to Allah)*, Allahu Akbar, alongside also practising Istighfar *(seeking forgiveness)*.
4. Practise gratitude and kindness to everybody and surround yourself with positive, like-minded, and kind-spirited people.
5. Listen to the Qur'aan - Surah Rahman, Surah Taha, Surah Al Baqarah, Surah Maryam, Surah Waqiah, Surah Ya-Sin, and Surah Al Kahf are my favourites.
6. Make amends with people you may need to build bridges with and do not hold grudges.
7. Motivate yourself through watching powerful lectures by

What difference did tahajjud make to my every day life?

reliable speakers/scholars/sheikhs.
8. Try to aim to pray tahajjud 1-2 times a week minimum.
9. Document your goals whatever they may be and reflect upon them regularly.
10. Practise acts that are a sunnah i.e having your hijama *(cupping)* done for extra rewards.
11. Read and learn all 99 names of Allah - pick the ones that resonate with you most and recite them often.
12. Practise self-ruqyah or listen to reliable audio's to cleanse and heal your spiritual state, mind, body and soul.

Narrated Aisha: "Once the Prophet ﷺ (peace be upon him) came while a woman was sitting with me. He said, "Who is she?" I replied, "She is so and so," and told him about her (excessive) praying. He said disapprovingly, "Do (good) deeds which is within your capacity (without being overtaxed) as Allah does not get tired (of giving rewards) but (surely) you will get tired and the best deed (act of Worship) in the sight of Allah is that which is done regularly." [Sahih al-Bukhari 43 - Book 2, Hadith 36]

Do I still pray tahajjud?

I get asked this question often. The straight forward answer is yes.

After three months of waking up for tahajjud every day, a whole hour before fajr, it had transformed my life and re-shifted my focus.

I felt renewed and ready to tackle life's curve-balls because I knew Allah was with me throughout my jihad *(struggle)*.

As I had initially started praying tahajjud for peace of mind and improved mental health, I no longer felt it was as necessary to wake up *every* night. The hours of little sleep I had accumulated over all of those weeks, really started to catch up with me. It was a strange feeling because I had become so attached to tahajjud prayer, that when it was time to almost somewhat let go of it, I felt really guilty. I always knew there would come a time that I would maybe not wake up every night, but I never realised just how much I would miss it. So much so that I still strive to wake up as often as I can regardless of how tired or busy my days are.

If I were to be honest and raw, aside from deprivation of sleep, I naturally reduced how much I was waking up for the simple fact that I was feeling happier. The result of several weeks of praying tahajjud had delivered its purpose. Du'aas were being answered, and new paths were presenting before me. I of course continued with fard salah, but over the summer of 2023, I had only woken up a handful of times for tahajjud. I like to see this in a positive light; that I was feeling so blessed and so content, that I didn't feel I needed to wake up for tahajjud as much, as Allah had given me so much of what I was asking for already. I was always in conversation with my Rab where-ever I would go because I had trained myself to make this a key component of my day.

Did I still make mistakes? Yes. Did I still sin? Yes. I am human, and we all will undoubtedly both consciously and unconsciously sin. What is utmost important is that you always seek forgiveness, and remember even when we fall short, our Rab's mercy is endless. Allah is Ar-Raheem *[The Most Merciful]*, Al-Kareem *[The Most Generous One].*

"Verily, Allah loves those who repent and those who purify themselves." Qur'aan, Surah Al Baqarah {2:222}

Unfortunately now looking back, for some part, I believe I was ignorant and naive in thinking this way. Should I have reduced the amount I was praying in the middle of night because Allah had already blessed me so much? To be honest, I should have continued to pray tahajjud minimum of 1-2 times a week for Allah is Al-Mu'akhkhir *[The Delayer]*. As quickly as something can be given to you, it also can be taken away. Sadly I did experience the harsh reality of this. I believe I had something taken away from me that I prayed for because of my ignorance. Do not become complacent. We are being tested every second of each day. We must remain steadfast and never deviate from the actual path of why we were created and placed on this earth.

Usāmah ibn Zayd ibn Hārithah (may Allah be pleased with him) reported: The Prophet's daughter sent for him to come over because her son was dying. The Prophet ﷺ (peace be upon him) sent her the greeting of peace and this message: "To Allah belongs what He takes, and to Him belongs what He gives, and for everything He sets a specific term. So she should have patience and seek the reward from Allah." [Al-Bukhari and Muslim]

I am a huge advocate for praying tahajjud for what your heart desires, but I also must stress that ultimately, the riches of the dunya will never equate to the riches of gaining closeness to Allah (SWT).

Upon reflection, this is where I most definitely fell short.

I never should have allowed the yearning of worldly gains overshadow my real purpose here.

My heart was broken *twice* this year. Friends and family have broken my heart, my own expectations have broken my heart, the dunya has broken my heart; through and through.

Do I still pray tahajjud?

I feel I have failed greatly.

It is easy to get caught up in the design of this dunya. It is incredibly easy to not only have your heart, but your mind broken too. However, if you give your heart to Allah (SWT), do you think it would break? When He is As-Salam *[The Source of peace]*, and Al-Barr *[The Source of Goodness]*?

"...put your trust in Allah, certainly, Allah loves those who put their trust (in Him)." Qur'aan, Surah Al-Imran {3:159}

Whenever you find yourself drawn toward the temptation of this dunya, make wudhu in the midst of the night and pray two rak'ats nafl.

Incorporate tahajjud into your weekly routine as I confidently have now.

Control your nafs *(self, ego, psyche)*. Do not allow the whisperings of shaitan manifest beyond your control for this temporary life.

Our ultimate goal should always be to strive to be a better Muslim, and remain attached to Allah and the Holy Qur'aan.

He said, "I only complain of my suffering and my grief to Allah, and I know from Allah that which you do not know." Qur'aan, Surah Yusuf {12:86}

One day in sha Allah, we will live forever in jannah where pain doesn't exist. Heartbreak doesn't exist. Temptation won't exist.

Evil won't exist.

Our hearts will return to our eternal home and we will dwell in seas of sakina *(tranquillity)*.

Abu Sa'id and Abu Hurairah (May Allah be pleased with them) reported: The Messenger of Allah ﷺ (peace be upon him) said, "When the dwellers of Jannah enter Jannah, an announcer will call: (You have a promise from Allah that) you will live therein and you will never die; you will stay healthy therein and you will never fall ill; you will stay young and you will never become old; you will be under a constant bliss and you will never feel miserable." [Al-Buhkari]

Were my du'aas really answered?

D u'aa is one of the most powerful tools a believer holds. The beauty of making du'aa really defines ones relationship with Al-Jaleel *[The Majestic One]*. During our communication with Allah, we are in open conversation directly with Him. No distractions, no interruptions. We are in special seclusion with Ash-Shaheed *[The All-Observing Witness]*, and we make du'aa with full conviction that Allah will of course, answer them.

Al-Nu'man ibn Bashir reported: The Prophet ﷺ (peace be upon him) said, "Supplication is worship itself." [Sunan at-Tirmidhi, 3247]

Then, the Prophet ﷺ (peace be upon him) recited the verse, "Your Lord said: Call upon Me and I will respond to you." Qur'aan, Surah Ghafir {40:60}

All my life, I was taught to raise my hands during du'aa not realising this is a sunnah, and not obligatory. When I learned I could make du'aa wherever I was and whenever I wanted, what do you think I did? I began making du'aa so frequently that more and more of them were being granted. It could have been the smallest of things, yet it was those smalls 'wins' that gave me fuel to keep persevering.

I would stop and make du'aa every single time it rained; whether it was made aloud or in my head.

I would write a list of du'aas before any planned travel or journey.

I would make du'aa during every sujood of every last rak'ah in my salah.

I would set reminders for the last hour of asr before maghreb, **every** jummuah to ensure I didn't miss that window of opportunity.

I memorised the following du'aa mentioned in the Qur'aan that Prophet Musa *(peace be upon him)* recited:

"Rabbi inni lima anzalta illayya min khayrin faqir."

This translates as, *"My Lord, Truly, I am in desperate need of the good You send me." Qur'aan, Surah Al Qasas {28:24}*

I recited this du'aa constantly throughout the day then, and still do all of the above now like clockwork. Whenever I recite this du'aa, I am instilling my submission to Allah and leaving my hopes and dreams *safely* with Him.

I depend on Him, and Him only.

The part I enjoy most about making du'aa? I needn't worry about raising my hands or being in a state of wudhu *(if you can then this is favourable of course)*. I have fallen in love with talking to my Rab whenever I need Him in both times of happiness, and grief. This has cemented my bond with Him. With every single du'aa I make, I become more and more reliant on my Maker.

He said, "I only complain of my suffering and my grief to Allah." Qur'aan, Surah Yusuf {12:86}

I was conscious of the fact that only Allah could relieve the deep sadness I was feeling, and so this is why it felt so satisfying as I was asking the only force that could invoke miracles for me. I was in desperate need of His 'kun faya kun' *('be and it is')*, and He never let me down. Not once.

"All it takes, when He wills something to be, is simply to say to it: "Be!" And it is!" Qur'aan, Surah Ya-Sin {36:82}

* * *

Allah's generosity is limitless.

When you are asking Him for what you desire, be specific, be detailed, and do not be shy.

Never become tired of making du'aa. Allah loves du'aas that are repeated.

There is shifa within making du'aa itself.

Ibn al-Qayyim (may Allah be pleased with him) said: "one of the most beneficial of remedies is persisting in du'aa." [Al-Daa' wa'l-Dawa' pg.25]

I can recall many du'aas of mine that were made and then instantaneously answered. I can also recall du'aas I made that were answered, but weeks and months after making them. I recall making du'aas that Allah has protected me from being answered, and it was this, that altered my thinking behind answered du'aas. Allahu Alam *(Allah knows best).*

You would have heard of the widely popular Quranic verse:

"But perhaps you hate a thing and it is good for you, and perhaps you love a thing and it is bad for you. Allah knows, while ye know not." Qur'aan, Surah Al-Baqarah {2:216}

At the beginning of this year, there was one du'aa in particular I was heavily making. I use the adjective heavily, because it would accurately describe how desperately and how often I was making this du'aa. It wasn't until several weeks down the line, was when it became clearly apparent why Allah had not answered it. I remember breaking down into sujood in gratitude of Allah's protection. I had come to a very harsh realisation of how Allah had blocked this du'aa being answered because He had my best interests at heart. I cried not because I was disheartened with the outcome, but instead I was joyous of how Allah made me wait patiently and sincerely, whilst He *gently* revealed why that du'aa I was making, wasn't what was actually good for me.

'Behind every delay there is khayr (goodness).' ~ Arabic Proverb

Allah is Al Hakeem *[The Wise]*, and I promise that if Allah is delaying, or seemingly not answering your du'aa, it is for a good reason. He will surely replace your wishes with dreams so beautiful, you would never imagine it to become your reality when it does.

Abu Sa'id al-Khudri reported: The Prophet ﷺ (peace be upon him) said, "There is no Muslim who calls upon Allah, without sin or cutting family ties, but that Allah will give him one of three answers: He will quickly fulfil his supplication, He will store it for him in the Hereafter, or He will divert an evil from him similar to it." They said, "In that case we will ask for more." The Prophet said, "Allah has even more." [Musnad Ahmad 11133 Sahih according to Al-Albani]

* * *

Tahajjud Du'aas

Tahajjud they say is by *invite only,* and I am in full agreement with this. There were many a time where I feel I wasn't sincere enough in wanting to wake up. It was those nights that I found it most difficult to wake up from my bed, and I would end up continuing to sleep. My niyyah wasn't genuine enough.

You will be invited by Al-Malik *[The King]* when He pleases and plans. He will make it easy for you. He will enable you to wake up as if you had already slept the whole night.

This is why I reiterate to not give up trying to wake up from your sleep; because when you do after all your persistence, the sweetness you will taste when you realise it was Allah Himself who woke you up and led you to Him, the feeling is like no other. The emotion is so full of love and peace, you can almost feel your soul residing in the lowest heaven with Him. *SubhanAllah.*

The way in which your Rab will reward your patience, will truly leave you speechless and in complete awe of Him.

Whilst the rest of the world sleeps, the doors of the skies are flown open between you and Him, Dhul-Jalali Wal Ikram *[The Lord of Majesty and Bounty].*

Many of my tahajjud du'aas have been answered *Alhamdulilah.* Not all, but many. Ones that I made for not only myself, but for others too.

It is for this very reason I call myself a 'tahajjud advocate'. My improved health and success stories, evidence that Allah performs His miracles through your remembrance in Him.

"And remember Me – I will surely remember you." Qur'aan, Surah Al Baqarah {2:152}

I am still working toward having one main du'aa in particular answered. I say working, because this is what I am doing. I am proving to Allah through acts of worship and devotion, that I am worthy of Him granting my most heartfelt du'aa.

Nothing worth having comes easy after all.

When I made Allah a core part of my everyday life, when I strived to pray all my fard salah, when I became gentle in my approach to life, when I practised sabr *(patience)* and maintained tawwakul *(trust in Allah)*, when I made time to read and listen to the Qur'aan, Allah blessed me differently. He then too remembered His tired slave, His broken slave, His slave that longed for His love.

When Allah makes you wait, do not ever think He does not hear the quiet whispers of your heart. He does.

He hears every single one.

"But they plan, and Allah plans. And Allah is the best of planners."
Qur'aan, Surah Al Imran {3:54}

Do not ever despair regardless of the hardships and obstacles you may be facing right now.

If I have not convinced you enough by now to pray tahajjud, I will make du'aa that every single person reading this…will in sha Allah.

I want everybody, especially those who feel broken by this

dunya to feel how I have felt throughout this journey of mine.

Every single time I pray tahajjud, I feel cradled by Allah's infinite love and mountains of mercy.

Tahajjud really does feed your soul; delicately filling every crevice of emptiness within your body with *pure* sakina.

Al Lateef *[The Most Gentle]* will never break your heart, so give your fragile heart to Him.

"The highest levels and ranks (in Jannah) are for someone who cries at night (to Allah) and smiles during the day (to people)." [Imam Dahabi Siyār a'lam an-Nubala, v.1, pg.141]

Tahajjud Testimonies

For those that follow me on TikTok, you would know in May this year, I asked for anyone who had a success story to share regarding their tahajjud journey to message me directly.

I thought of many ways to end this book, and I could think of no better way than ending it with countless accounts of tahajjud success stories to not only motivate you further, but for you to fall in love with Allah's 'kun faya kun' right before your own eyes.

I have of course, kept each testimony anonymous.

Trigger warning as you may find some of the following testimonies distressing

***

Testimony One

"I prayed tahajjud once and this was a couple months ago, even before I started praying salah or getting closer to Allah. What is crazy is that I feel like just that once, changed a lot for me. Me and my dad's family don't really get on. I suppose it's hard for him to understand because it's his family. I guess I get upset because I expect him to understand my point of view as I am his daughter. Something happened and we had a disagreement in regards to his sisters daughter which left me really really upset, and I was devastated and very very heartbroken. I was really upset. I spent days crying and feeling emotionally broken. I didn't speak to my dad (for the first time by the way) for days in the hope that he would see how emotionally damaging the situation was for me. I hoped he'd understand and see because I'm his daughter, I should be most valuable to him which I am, but somehow he was blinded when it came to his family. So I didn't speak to him, he did not speak back to me either. I was down for days, I believe almost two weeks in which I had even fallen ill. I honestly felt so broken and I just did not know what to do. My husband tried helping me and despite him trying effortlessly, and me even wanting to be okay just for his sake, I still felt so upset and would consistently cry. Then one night I said to my husband I want to pray, I want to pray to Allah because it is impossible for me to try and even explain the slightest of how I'm feeling, but without having to explain much Allah knows, He knows what I'm going through. It was quite late at night and Alhamdulilah luckily for me, it was tahajjud time. So I had done my wudhu and I prayed my rak'ahs, I'm not sure how many but it wasn't much. All I remember is crying and crying and crying throughout the entire prayer, and pouring my heart out to Allah and telling Him I know He knows how I feel; only He knows fully and understands. I asked Him to help me I told Him how painful it was and I just cried. I then went to sleep and instantly I felt peace, it was weird because I didn't fully acknowledge it at first, but Alhamdulilah I felt somewhat content and relaxed. I was still sad but somewhat lighter, and as days went by I think it was just a couple days, me and my dad also started talking again despite the situation not really being resolved, and honestly that is down to Allah. Alhamdulilah, after a short while I started recognising that it was because of tahajjud. Till now when I think about how quickly Allah (SWT) heard me and helped me, it amazes me. It was honestly a situation I felt like I wouldn't be able to get out of, and just like that within a few days of praying to Him, and asking Him for help, I was okay. I think that is also something that brought me closer to Allah Alhamdulilah! I just pray…I can carry on practising Islam properly, and pray on time as well. I also incorporate tahajjud a lot more."

How tahajjud saved my life.

* * *

Testimony Two

"Last Ramadaan I applied for a promotion and was successful, but didn't get offered it where I wanted it. I have a little boy and knew if I took it, I would struggle…so I started praying tahajjud. We needed the money and I didn't know what to do. Alhamdulilah a week later I got an email with an even better offer which worked perfectly around my family. SubhanAllah I tell you on that day Allah (SWT) was showing me His miracles."

* * *

Testimony Three

"Last year around this time, my husband of 28 years left me. We have a disabled son who is 20 years old. I begged for him to come back. I was on my own, and with very little money. I was at home trying to figure things out. Everyone blocked me, and whoever I would speak to could not say any more than to pray and ask for a miracle. As I could not confide in anyone, and had no-one to listen to me, I started with du'aas then salah. I figured out when to read tahajjud. I cried, and cried asking Allah (SWT) to see me through this. Either bring my husband back, or sort something for me where by it would be best for myself and my son. I asked Allah to lead and show me a way. More than anything else, patience was key. I in anger would say, 'Allah if you are there then show me.' I first gained inner peace, and then slowly things started to work one by one…"

* * *

Testimony Four

"My tahajjud success story goes like this. I finished university in December of 2021, Alhamdulilah. I had absolutely no idea on how to transition from university life to the world of work. By the time the middle of February 2022 came, I was up almost every night until 4am searching all the corners of the internet for job applications, and applying to every and any job I possibly could. I had become depressed and it was a really dark time for me. I questioned my worth and my choice of study. Everything just seemed to not be working out. One early morning as I was looking for job applications, I thought to myself, 'you know, you're up every night at this time, stressing and crying and tirelessly searching for work, yet Allah is HERE. He has descended every night for you to simply ASK Him. Why haven't you?' As I write this, tears are running down my face at the shear miracle of it. Some would call this unbelievable, but I left everything, made my wudhu, and prayed two rak'ah for tahajjud at about 3:30am on a Thursday night/morning. I cried, but I did not beg. I simply told

How tahajjud saved my life.

Allah I was tired of feeling hopeless. Could He please grant me a job, whatever it may be., and I left it at that whilst continuing my job search. The next day, Friday, a class mate of mine put in the class group that a huge corporate company in my country was looking for a photographer urgently, and that if anyone was interested they should put their name forward. I had studied Fine Art Photography, so clearly this was in my field of work. I was doubting myself though. I thought I wasn't a good enough photographer to take the leap for such a big company, but the smallest voice somewhere in the back on my mind said 'just do it. It doesn't hurt to just put your name forward. It'll either be a yes or a no.' I gave my name to the classmate, she forwarded it and I let it be. I must've forgot about it that weekend because when Monday came around I got a phone call and it was the company…after a 15 minute speed interview I was hired as a product photographer on an indefinite contract basis. ALHAMDULILAH! ALLAH IS GREAT! I am no longer a photographer, but I am in a different more developmental role in the same company for the same manager as she saw potential in me to work in communications. So now I am doing a graduate program as a product communications coordinator, with the potential to become permanent. I am so grateful Alhamdulilah for all that Allah has granted me. But I am mostly grateful for the tests of sabr that He constantly gives me. That's only one story, but it's the most significant in my life so far, Alhamdulilah."

* * *

Testimony Five

"I'm a single mum of two children. One of my children is severely disabled, and for that reason I was in real need of a bigger house to cater for her needs. I prayed tahajjud at the beginning of Ramadaan and made so much du'aa to Allah that He provides me and my kids with a new home that is perfect for us. Wallahi I kid you not, within the first week of Ramadaan, Allah blessed me with a home in the area I wanted it, and Alhamdulilah we are all settled and well. Allah is the best of planners and listens to every du'aa, Alhamdulilah."

* * *

Testimony Six

"I am the youngest of three elder brothers, but the eldest girl in my extended family. Growing up from a strict family who would chose culture over Islam in many cases other than for themselves, meant it was very hard and painful growing up. However, as I grew up to the age of 15, I had met someone and I had prayed istikhara for him and Alhamdulilah up till this date, it is still going strong. However years went by and I am now 20 years old, but at the age of 18 I've always wanted to get my nikkah done as young as possible as I knew that Allah (SWT) has given me so much guidance and signs that this man was the one. So one point of my life it was Ramadaan and his family approached me saying that they would like to come ask for my hand. I was very scared because my family did not understand the concept of getting married young and making it halal. However it was the time of Ramadaan, and it was the last ten days. I was told by his family I need to speak to one of my parents. Of course you can imagine how scary it was knowing that no one in my family had ever gotten married from outside of the family before. On one of the odd nights I'm presuming the 23rd night, I prayed tahajjud that 'ya Allah give me the courage to tell my father about this, and if me and him are meant to be make it easy for me to tell him.' That very same day I still can't remember the moment due to how scared I was, I told my father and he didn't react to it in a bad way, but till this day I'm fighting to get my nikkah done. The point of this tahajjud story is that my du'aa got accepted the very first day, and till this day I'm shocked that my father knows. May Allah make it easy for me as I am still continuing on with the battle Ameen."

* * *

Testimony Seven

"My now husband reverted to Islam, and during that time we went to Islamic classes at the mosque. This was where I went on to meet other reverts that totally moved me and inspired me - I felt like a revert. I knew nothing about my deen. As time went on my now husband reverted to Islam, and I became solid in my salah. I eventually told my parents who I wanted to marry. Coming from a Pakistani background, they weren't happy. I love my family and would never leave them for anyone, so I started praying tahajjud - Alhamdulilah with all my tears, du'aas, and efforts of getting up in middle of night for tahajjud (which I super struggled with), my dad six months later accepted, and we got married. My dad and husband are now best buds!"

* * *

Testimony Eight

"During Ramadaan I had woken up for tahajjud and my head was hurting so much. It felt like an awful migraine and I felt very ill from it. I prayed two rak'ahs. In the first sujood I asked Allah to please remove my migraine. As I stood up from the first sujood, my migraine slowly subsided and it was gone Alhamdulilah. I couldn't stop crying at Allah's mercy. Alhamdulilah."

* * *

Testimony Nine

"In March 2023, I prayed for five days before my driving test to pass (this was my second time going for the test). I passed the test! Also to add it was a very easy test. The examiner was super nice and helped me a lot. He said to me I can go when I was hesitating, and also said to me well done when I squeezed through some gaps which was encouraging, as you know examiners don't usually make comments like this. The best part of it all was that my test was 32 minutes long, instead of the full 40 minutes."

* * *

Testimony Ten

"In January 2016, my marriage ended to someone I loved very much. On February 26th 2016, I lost my sister who was my best friend. I immersed myself in worshipping Allah. I was extremely broken and prayed tahajjud every single day. I was also not allowed to see my kids at all. In 2018, I lost my mother. I was still not allowed access to my kids. I kept making du'aa to be reunited with them, and for Allah to soften their mother's heart. Today, we have become best friends and I have full access to my children. I also have healed completely and achieved so many other miracles spiritually and otherwise. I continue with tahajjud and enjoy the most profound relationship with Allah! Alhamdulilah."

* * *

Testimony Eleven

"I started university with no intention of falling for someone or find someone because that's just not the way it works with my family. I had no problem with that, but then it just happened. This man caught my eye, and then I noticed something happening between us; the constant eye contact. My friends noticed too. It was like we had a connection. I started to notice all his good habits and I felt a deeper connection. I just had this feeling that it was mutual, and I fell for him. This wasn't the way things were supposed to go, and I almost lost complete faith because my family would never agree to it. I prayed tahajjud one night. I asked Allah to give me a sign that this man is meant for me, and for Allah to take the feelings I have for this man out of my heart if he's not the one written for me. The following day Allah gave me a sign. It happened in the most beautiful way because I had forgotten I'd even made du'aa for a sign, and when I saw it that's what my mind jumped to, SubhanAllah. I also prayed istikhara prior to this as well, and there was nothing but positive feelings and good signs. It's

Testimony Eleven

like Allah gave me the signs, He's told me 'look I've shown you what is yours, you just need to trust My timing and that I will give you what is meant for you when you are ready for it.' Ever since then I always pray that my family's mindset changes by the time it comes to my marriage in sha Allah, and I still make du'aa that if he's not meant for me, then take the feelings I have for him out of my heart. I made this du'aa bawling my eyes fully in tears to our Lord, and He heard me and He gave me signs upon signs…this is the power of tahajjud prayer. It will all work out in its own time, this whole process has shown me that we just need to have blind faith in Allah and trust his timings for He is the best of planners SubhanAllah."

* * *

Testimony Twelve

"Around two years ago, I left an abusive marriage with three children. Mentally I was really disturbed and was so timid and scared around everyone; as you know within the Asian community it was not liked, and my parents were encouraging me to go back to my mums. I didn't blame them. They wanted the best for me and didn't want me to suffer. I was crying and begging for them to not send me back, however my ex-husband was very clever and was showing my mother his best side. I could see through it all and knew it was all an act to get me to go back. I could see no other way than to ask Allah (SWT) for help. I prayed tahajjud almost every day. I cried and begged Allah to show me the right way, and if what I'm doing is right for my mum to agree to let me apply for divorce. She was so against divorce, I thought she'd never agree and I'd be stuck with this man forever. I could see no hope, but carried on praying as much as I could, and one day out of the blue after some events had happened with my ex-husband and his family, my mum who was so against my divorce, encouraged me to go and get a divorce. She saw the truth, and saw through the lies. It was nothing less than a miracle for me. So many years of wanting to leave, and so many tears and arguments and she finally agreed. Alhamdulilah my parents have supported me so much since, but I do believe that this all happened because of my prayers and tahajjud. If I didn't do that, maybe I would still be stuck with an abusive man and I might not have been here today, but Alhamdulilah for everything."

* * *

Testimony Thirteen

"I found out I had a blood clot in my heart and I was terrified. I started reaching out to Allah in salah and started praying tahajjud. Doctors were trying to figure out how to get rid of this blood clot through maybe going in and breaking it up, or giving me medicines. I started praying tahajjud without fail, and prayed to Allah to get rid of it before they did something. I then went for my heart scan to see where this blood clot was and was told it had disappeared! SubhanAllah! Just like that! After this, they had discharged me as I no longer needed any treatment."

* * *

Testimony Fourteen

"I prayed tahajjud about a person I was speaking to and for some reason I said in my du'aa that if this person was good for me, I asked Allah to make our relationship stronger and more easy. I also asked that if they weren't good for me, for us to not talk to each other anymore. But because of my love towards them, I knew I couldn't be the one to end it so I asked if we couldn't stop talking to each other, make it so they would be the one to end it. Shortly after she started having doubts and after a few weeks she ended up leaving. So it was a very powerful and effective du'aa I made."

* * *

Testimony Fifteen

"I must admit I'm not a regular five times a day salah girl, and I wasn't at the time of this story. Without going into too much detail, a close family member had gotten arrested and had to spend time in prison (through no fault of their own). It was an incredible shock, completely unexpected, happened on a very random day and for the first time, I was desperate and could turn to no one but Allah to help in that situation. It was something that had never previously happened, and the fear for that person was overwhelming. I prayed to my Lord and woke up for tahajjud and six weeks later, that person came home. The initial reason for the arrest was definitely not small or minor, and ordinarily that person would still be in prison. I believe my Lord answered my du'aa, and I will forever be grateful. Since then I have prayed for something else (marriage to a specific person), and I'm still waiting for that du'aa to be accepted. I know I'm not an amazing Muslim and I have a lot of work to do. I will always be grateful to Allah for accepting my first du'aa, and accepting anything else is a bonus for a sinner like me who

Testimony Fifteen

doesn't deserve this much mercy/kindness."

***

Testimony Sixteen

"I swear by tahajjud. I would not be where I am today without praying tahajjud. I was in an 11 year marriage. I'd pray, pouring my heart out and praying for Allah to make my ex, love and care for me and my son. I'd spend all night praying nafl, fasting for him to be mine, love me and care for me and my son. I completed hajj, umrah's...I was a mess. I used to pray tahajjud...hit and miss not regularly; just prayed it every now and then. The day my ex divorced me, I was fasting for the sake of him changing towards me after the divorce. I did not know how to do du'aa, because all I ever did was pray for him. So one day I watched a YouTube video on tahajjud and it made me think that if this elderly women (the YouTuber) with health conditions can pray tahajjud, why can't I? She talked about how she prayed tahajjud and Qur'aan before fajr. From that day on, I made tahajjud apart of my routine and my ten year old son also prayed it now and then. The trauma my son went through and how he struggled, was just as bad as how I was affected. Nearly four years on, and my son is a different

Testimony Sixteen

child and me, I don't even remember what my ex looks like. My son doesn't remember his fathers name. The father divorced me and tried tarnishing my reputation. Where I could have taken revenge or told the whole world my side of the story, I went quiet and cried during tahajjud. I'd talk to Allah about everything I endured and how Allah witnessed everything, and how I solely relied on my Lord. Allah unfolded stuff without me uttering a word. I'd see little miracles every day. From the woman who lost everything, wasn't able to look after her own child, had social services on my case too…to today, supporting other women and advising others. Tahajjud is my victory, my strength, my go to comfort of the week. When I'm not able to pray it, life feels empty. People ask what therapy they should have, what activity should they take up to help them heal, I say tahajjud is your therapy, tahajjud is your activity and if I am saying this, I'm saying it for a reason. I was at deaths door. My life was nothing but darkness. What I did to heal is pray tahajjud."

* * *

Testimony Seventeen

"My tahajjud success story was more of the kind where I had to continuously pray regularly and consistently to see any sort of effect. At one point I thought of giving up, and felt so demotivated but SubhanAllah, during that time it was Ramadaan and I kept getting reminders to pray and make du'aa because ultimately, du'aa is the most powerful weapon we have and it can change qadr. Allah (SWT) wouldn't allow you to raise your hands up and beg him for something so badly if he didn't want you to have it. Allah would never leave you empty handed and SubhanAllah this really allowed me to keep pushing as well as teaching me patience. My dad's side of the family were so close knit Allah humma barek. All my life I'd seen them get along, and they truly were such a big part of my life. An incident occurred November 2021 which made my father cut ties with his side of the family. It was a huge deal for me as I felt completely lost in that time. I fell into a depressive state where I closed myself off to everyone. I didn't want to communicate, nor be around people anymore.

Testimony Seventeen

My whole life took a U-turn, and on top of that, I had no contact with my biggest support system, my family. Since I was so close to them, it affected me massively. I remember nights crying myself to sleep because of how unfortunate the situation was. Nobody was ever the same. Eid's and festivities were never the same. I decided to start praying tahajjud for Allah (SWT) to reconcile and reunite my family back together. I prayed and prayed and prayed, countless nights in prayer, begging Allah (SWT) to mend my broken family and resolve these family affairs, for Allah (SWT) is the Best Disposer of affairs. Alhamdulilah, after a year and a half of turmoil and constant battle, my family are now reunited. I haven't seen my father and his siblings get along like this in so long Allah humma barek. I am finally able to spend time with my cousins who were like sisters to me without any worries or tension. I know we still have a long way to go, but Alhamdulilah I couldn't be more grateful. This tahajjud story took a while, but by the mercy of Allah (SWT), He accepted my du'aas in bringing my family together as one, and blessing us with one another once again. This was my first, and most recent tahajjud to be accepted. One which was answered with time and consistency."

* * *

Testimony Eighteen

"I have two distinct stories, one of which I saw the effect of tahajjud instantaneously within hours, and another which took a longer period of time to get accepted. I'll start with my first ever tahajjud I prayed. This was the morning of my driving test. I was so nervous and it was a huge deal for me, hence why I decided to pray tahajjud and Alhamdulilah I passed the same day. This may seem like a small one, but it was the first tahajjud I'd ever offered back in 2018 and it stuck with me."

* * *

Testimony Nineteen

"I have a story about a time where I was working whilst going to college, and I was praying my five a day salah, not tahajjud as much but I was getting stronger on my deen. I felt the connection with Allah, an unbreakable bond. One day a negative situation at work had led me to leaving. I had piles of course work whilst juggling a job from 8-6pm, and when I had gone home that day, I was going to tell my mum but something stopped me. It was as though Allah was trying to tell me not to tell others and to speak to Him only. So I had prayed tahajjud that night and poured my heart out. I felt the stress slowly fading as I told Allah everything. I then had gone to college that same day, and was given a way out which was an apprenticeship opportunity. As I stayed on the path of apprenticeship, fast forward to now, I have seen many greater job placements. I've been placed in far better positions from what was taken and I am ever so grateful. It was as if Allah had made me a promise that from that day onwards, I am to receive something far better. The journey wasn't easy, but from the job

I had gone to today, really made me look back and think wow indeed it was like a promise fulfilled. After that day I believe everything happens for a reason Allah is Al-Mu'id, The One who remoulds, replaces, and renews. Allah has taught me this over and over, and I am in love with it. Something has to take the place of something else sometimes, otherwise you cannot find something new. Anything we have lost in life has only created space for something more valuable."

* * *

Testimony Twenty

"I prayed tahajjud for eight years to help in an unsuccessful marriage. I got married out of despite. I never lived with the guy. I prayed everyday to Allah (SWT) to show me the right path. If I should go on with the marriage or get divorced. It was a hard, tough journey. I believe Allah (SWT) answered my tahajjud prayers. The other fact was just my parents not wanting me to be divorced which took a whole three years of convincing. However, Alhamdulilah the day I got my signs from Allah (SWT), I put my own effort in and made it till the end. At times I felt to give up, nothing was happening or moving forward, but I never forgot that this was the path Allah wanted me to take, and that marriage although I wish it never happened, it taught me a lot. It taught me patience, the qadr of du'aa/prayer, and strong belief in Allah (SWT)."

* * *

Testimony Twenty-One

"I am 24 years old. I have felt stuck in my family home my whole life. Abusive environment. Mentally and emotionally. Mum left once when I was a child, and again when I was 22. I am the only daughter with two younger brothers (18 and 21, but they act worse than a 3 year old throwing tantrums.) There was a lot of pressure on me to cook and clean, maintain the house etc. Whilst doing my masters, and processing that my mum betrayed me again. I spent this Ramadaan praying tahajjud almost every night begging Allah that by next Ramadaan, I would have moved out into my own home. SubhanAllah a week or two after Ramadaan ended, I did an interview and got into a funded PhD programme that is based outside of London. So now Alhamdulilah I'm able to move out and afford it because it is not in London; at the end of the three years, I will have a PhD in sha Allah."

* * *

Testimony Twenty-Two

"I was in an abusive relationship for eight years, my husband left me exactly two months after burying my still-born son. He left me as a form of punishment, because 'I had lost his son'. A year later, he refused to divorce me, again as a form of punishment. Nothing was working for me, no mediation from family elders etc. Someone mentioned a shariah council to me, I contacted them, and also started praying tahajjud. By the will of Allah, the second day I prayed tahajjud, he accepted my initiation of divorce."

* * *

Testimony Twenty-Three

"I began praying tahajjud during Ramadan this year as I was experiencing many issues within my marriage. SubhanAllah, not only did it ease my worries as I was continuously crying every day, not eating and sleeping, but it also gave me clarity. Slowly but surely, I found ease with prayer. My heart had been detached from my husband. I was lost and I didn't know what to ask for. I just prayed to Allah that He did whatever was best for me as I had tawwakul in Him. Everything I prayed for just happened SubhanAllah. In sha Allah I am going through the khula process soon."

* * *

Testimony Twenty-Four

"It was my first time praying tahajjud, this was around the middle of October I think. I woke up and made my du'aa after tahajjud. I didn't pray it correctly I feel because I didn't know much about it at that time. I made du'aa to get accepted for a part-time job that I needed to support myself alongside my university degree. I had the interview already, and I was now just waiting for a phone call or an email. In the afternoon on the same day, I got a call from the employer to say I got the job. I had already been waiting for a few days, so I'm certain I only got that call due to praying tahajjud. I've been praying tahajjud every so often now."

* * *

Testimony Twenty-Five

"Personally, my experience relates to my mother's death in 2021 from Covid. I gave up all hope on life, wanted to end it many times. My relationship was over 10 years long, and it had ended too due to my own trauma and religion. I found Allah, and I found a piece of myself through tahajjud that was missing. I started to become a believer in the akhirah and Allah's promise for Muslims, and here I am today, standing stronger, taller than ever before. I am my mothers sadaqah jaariyah, and everyday I send her a gift through prayer. I live by this: The wait will show you that everything happened for a reason. That's the love of Allah."

***

Testimony Twenty-Six

"I was speaking to someone who I started speaking to with the intention of marriage. My family found out and made me cut contact with him, and also made me cut contact with my friends etc. I was not able to speak to any of my friends or him for a full year. Luckily Covid hit and everyone was on lockdown so I didn't feel like the only one in lockdown due to my family finding out. I turned to Allah and begged him to make this person good for me, and make me good for this person also. I continuously prayed tahajjud regularly, and then a year later me and him got in contact through email at first, and then got families involved. We ended up getting married and now I am happily married with a one year old Alhamdulilah. Allah works in mysterious ways and we had lost all hope after being away from each other, but then Allah made it all happen Alhamdulilah."

* * *

Testimony Twenty-Seven

"My tahajjud story is that I was married to an abusive narcissistic man who I felt deep inside was cheating on me. Every time I questioned him, I would get called crazy and other horrible names. He was constantly gas lighting me. I wasn't the type to spy or go down his phone, so I prayed tahajjud. Literally within a week, Allah gave me solid proof of what he was getting up to behind my back, cheating with different women who all knew about me. I left with my two kids, but then was left homeless for seven months. I was praying tahajjud during this difficult time. In January this year, I finally secured my own place for me and girls in the best location. I am now building a safe home for me and my two girls. I went through therapy which really helped Alhamdulilah. I couldn't be more grateful to Allah for everything. My divorce went through today and I couldn't be happier Alhamdulilah."

Testimony Twenty-Seven

***

Testimony Twenty-Eight

"So I ran into one of your TikTok posts about tahajjud in Ramadaan . Think I may have even said in the comments that I will give it a go. Anyway one day I did pray it in Ramadaan. I was up and thought might as well. At the time I had left my job and was looking for a software engineer job. I asked for it in the tahajjud. What do you know it worked and I ended up with the job before Ramadaan even ended."

* * *

Testimony Twenty-Nine

"In January I was going through a lot...my world was crumbling. I'm a single mum to an autistic nine year old, and honestly things got really bad. I cried for days, all day! Breakdowns at the gym and pouring my heart out in sujood. I recorded a video of myself crying so I would never ever forget that moment, and to remind myself that I never wanted to be that weak again...Tahajjud helped a lot. I didn't get what I wanted straight away, but during Ramadan, 23 months later, Alhamdulilah Allah replaced all with far better beyond what I ever imagined. I was trying to finish the Qur'aan, and Allah attached my heart more in seeking wisdom and processing the Qur'aan (with English translation). This benefited me a lot. I started to implement all these other things like Islamic podcasts...WALLAH they taught me so much Alhamdulilah, and slowly I was in a place where I felt loved by Allah...like one of His favourites. Tahajjud was like reassurance for me, Allah will come through with better. I'd rather stay lonely and close to my deen, than with company and away from my Lord, and

How tahajjud saved my life.

Allah knows best. He is the best of all planners. You haven't lost anything until you've lost your deen, so regardless of how much it fluctuates, I run back every chance I get because I'm so scared of being apart from my Lord. I know what it's like for Allah to seal your eyes and heart and I never wanna go back there again. He truly guides who He wills. Since working towards my deen, I've never felt mentally and physically this good. Tahajjud kept me steady in having tawwakul, sabr, and trusting the qadr of Allah. The conversations between me and Allah are so casual, I sometimes just talk to Him like He is my best friend; I feel like those conversations are more heard than structured du'aas. The days I lay on my prayer mat after salah, I felt like Allah was hugging me. I would fall asleep and I'd remember every bit of comfort I got through the madness I went through. There truly is khayr (goodness) in every struggle SubhanAllah..Allah was always there. We should never forget where we've come from, and never forget how quickly this 'happiness/contentment' can be taken away if you're not appreciative enough."

* * *

Testimony Thirty

"There was a job that I really wanted and I made du'aa for it. I even woke up for tahajjud for it, but in the du'aa I said to Allah only give me this job if there is khayr in it, but if there is no khayr in it, then I am certain You will give me something better. The next day I got an email saying I didn't get the job however the day after that, I got an email about a job opportunity whereby SubhanAllah, they extended their deadline and so I was able to apply after seeing the email. I applied to it and I got the job. Alhamdulilah it was amazing and I love the job so much!"

* * *

Testimony Thirty-One

"I used to go to an Islamic boarding school when I was in my teens and we had really tough end of year exams. I wasn't the most dedicated student as a teenager, but I always wanted to pass the year to make my mum happy. During exams, everyone would be awake revising continuously and praying tahajjud and making du'aa at accepted times etc. One of the years I hadn't been able to revise properly juggling between GCSEs, an Islamic education. I also hadn't worked very hard throughout the year, but I prayed so hard at tahajjud in the weeks leading up to exams. I begged Allah to make me pass even though I didn't deserve it, but for the sake of making my parents happy. It was due to their efforts and sacrifices that I was studying there. And honestly, I really don't know how, but I passed the year. This might not seem so crazy, but I had days during those exams where I would come out feeling deflated because of how bad some of them went. My classmates would discuss the paper answers after and I would overhear them. My heart would sink knowing how bad I thought I had done, but with my du'aas made at tahajjud, I don't know how, but I passed. Those studies were difficult - it's true that the the dua made at tahajjud is like an arrow that never misses it's target and I stand by this 100%."

* * *

Testimony Thirty-Two

"I got married in 2018 and I wasn't getting pregnant. I had tried seeing doctors, but nothing was helping. Fast forward to 2021, I attended an itikaf program in a masjid that included tahajjud prayers. This included praying from 9pm starting taraweeh, all the way to 5am throughout the night for the longest tahajjud prayers I had ever witnessed in my whole life. This imaam took no breaks. He was praying extremely long sujoods, and ruk'uhs, and the surahs recited were very long. I found myself in this great opportunity, in these long instances, to make the most du'aa I could think of, and literally just speak to my Lord. I spoke to my Lord and I asked him for a child during this whole entire time in the last ten days of Ramadaan in itikaf (whilst staying in the masjid). I came out from that itikaf and after Eid, six weeks passed that I had miss my period. Something miraculously told me to go inside and do a pregnancy test at the doctors because my heart just knew. Guess what… it was positive. After five long years of a childless marriage, Allah listened to my du'aa just like that. He granted me a beautiful son just like I asked him, and I have named him Ibrahim…just like I was telling myself I would in those long sujoods. I really realised Allah (SWT) is so much more closer to us than we think, and He is so Merciful to us. Please please do not underestimate the power of tahajjud. It is like an arrow that doesn't miss it's target. I thanked Allah so much and just I cried and fell into prostration. Alhamdulilah ya Rab, I am so grateful."

***

Testimony Thirty-Three

"When I was pregnant in the first trimester, I had this gut feeling that my husband was cheating. I had zero proof, and I didn't want to make an accusation as it is haram. I did drop little comments without making an accusation, and I was called crazy and that my hormones were getting the best of me. At this point I decided to pray tahajjud. Months later when I was seven months pregnant, he told me that he went for training for work. I still had this gut feeling inside me, but again, I didn't have any proof. He called me to say goodnight, and he said he was in bed going to sleep. I then received a call from him two minutes later and it was him, but this time he accidentally called me and the stuff I heard confirmed he was 110% cheating. When he came home the next day and I questioned him, he then called me crazy again and said I must have been dreaming. Even after I showed him the call register, he said there's something wrong with my phone because he had deleted his call register, and kept insisting his phone was right. I left it there and kept my trust in Allah and that He would bring proof forward that he couldn't lie his way out of. So I continued to pray tahajjud and didn't give up hope in Allah. At this point, I had given birth and only a few weeks after I had her, I saw in his phone that there was a video of him confirming cheating. I sent the video to my phone for proof. He had no choice but to admit it and we had gotten into an argument which got physical. My older daughter called the police once they got involved, I soon found out from his criminal records that he was on the sex offenders list. He had raped two little boys and been to prison for it prior. The social workers got involved and I had to get a restraining order. I'm so grateful to Allah for saving me and my daughters from an evil man like this Alhamdulilah."

* * *

Testimony Thirty-Four

"Years into my marriage, we were finding it difficult to settle into our own home with our two daughters. We relocated so many times between London and the North of England. We lived with my in-laws and my own family back and fourth. It was a horrible cycle as we never felt we belonged anywhere. It was a relentlessly tiring time having to constantly reshuffle our lives, change my children's schools etc. After my husband and I prayed tahajjud, we were able to secure our first family home. We finally now feel settled, and my daughters too are so happy Alhamdulilah."

* * *

Testimony Thirty-Five

"For four years I was working in a job where I was always heavily stressed and overworked. My work load was increasing, but our team wasn't. I enjoyed my job so I didn't want to actually leave. No matter how much I asked for support or more staff, everything stayed stuck. I also felt no-one was seeing I was drowning in stress from the job. I specifically prayed tahajjud for recognition in my role, a team, and more money. Within two weeks of praying tahajjud for this, the CEO came to find me. He offered me a managerial role, a pay rise, and provided me with a team."

* * *

Testimony Thirty-Six

"My sister has been in a marriage of over ten years with one son. She suffers with mental health disorders and other physical health issues. Her in-laws exacerbate her symptoms and bully her in her own home. My sister asked for me to pray tahajjud for her to get her own place. I also told her to pray tahajjud for this so it would be more powerful. Fast forward seven months, she is now decorating her new home ready to move in soon."

* * *

Testimony Thirty-Seven

"My cousin-sister really wanted to get pregnant. She was newly married and in her late thirties so she was very conscious of this. There was a very small time frame in which she could conceive in this particular situation. I longed to see my cousin-sister pregnant as we are so close. I wanted to witness her become a mother so I prayed tahajjud for this. She has supported me so much emotionally so this was the least I could do for her. Within three months, she became pregnant in circumstances you wouldn't think possible. Allahu Akbar!! I believe my tahajjud du'aas helped!"

***

Testimony Thirty-Eight

"Like everyone else, I only used to read tahajjud for very important du'aas or if I had something I desperately needed to happen. However as I started praying more and getting to closer to Allah, I was reading tahajjud almost every night; particularly when there were marriage talks with my *now* husband. I asked Allah for my nikkah to be a blessing and for us to be happy and content with one another. Every tahajjud, I asked for a list of small things. Alhamdulilah we've been married for five years, and we have continued tahajjud for the smallest of things. During my pregnancy, we also prayed tahajjud for a healthy pregnancy, and for a good birth. Everything I asked for, Allah granted in good time and sometimes I got **more** than I even asked for. Tahajjud has definitely been a prayer where my du'aas have been arrows that haven't missed their targets."

* * *

Testimony Thirty-Nine

"I requested Allah to grant me my wife through tahajjud. We weren't married at that time and I repeated that du'aa. After around six months, our marriage date was fixed."

***

Testimony Forty

"I have longed to find my companion for years. My real search started in 2017. Every time I would speak to someone for marriage, they would leave after a few months and completely change their mind about me. This repeated with two further potentials. I prayed and begged Allah for a person to enter my life specifically after Ramadaan who would be everything I was looking for. Unexpectedly, I came across somebody who I clicked with instantly. I was scared throughout the whole duration we were speaking as I was waiting for it to go wrong. Although we no longer speak, I felt this situation was different. I feel this person is the person I have asked for due to the nature of how different it was throughout, and the exact time he came into my life. He brought laughter to my days. I felt cared for and wanted. I had never experienced this with previous potentials. I got to experience how it was like for someone to actually be interested in me, even though it was seemingly short-lived. We are not completely out of each others lives and I believe there is still hope. Every time I pray tahajjud and ask Allah to keep us connected or show me a sign, He has given me it within a matter of hours/days of me asking SubhanAllah. I believe Allah is delaying our reunion for a good reason. I will continue to pray tahajjud until Allah grants my wishes to reconnect with him again in sha Allah. I know that patience is key…and I will wait for him."

Afterword

For those that know and have known me, you would know poetry and literature have always been close to my heart ever since I was a little girl.

I loved reading, borrowing, and buying books and started writing my own stories when I was six years old. I sought solace in escaping reality and diving deep into my own imagination. As I grew older and into my teens, my passion for literature took a different turn and instead, I began writing poetry to channel my grief of losing my *beloved* mother at the time. Poetry was a means of healing for me, and I had always dreamed of becoming a published author of either a novel, or a book consisting of a collection of my own poems.

During Covid-19, I started writing my own fantasy romance novel which really ignited my passion for writing again. I wrote a few chapters, but unfortunately never attempted to finish it or see it through to the end.

When I had the idea of typing my own account of my tahajjud

Afterword

journey as a book, I couldn't help but think of the dream that little Saba once had of becoming a recognised, and published author.

This was never a du'aa I had ever intentionally made, but one that I had always secretly kept in my heart.

Now I sit here, with tears rolling down my face, coming to the realisation that Allah has answered this du'aa without me even asking for it.

All those years ago, Allah knew.

He knew that not only was He was going to answer this du'aa, but in the most beautiful, beautiful of ways.

No, it isn't a romance fiction novel He had written for me to share with the world, but the most perfect tale of my love story between me and Him.

I am so grateful. So humbled. So content.

My Rab answered a du'aa I didn't even see coming. Alhamdulilah.

Al-Mussawir *[The Flawless Shaper]*, Al-Muktadir *[The Determiner]*, Al-Mujeeb *[The Responding One]*.

You would have noticed throughout the chapters that I have included many of Allah's precious names. Learning and reciting all 99 names of Allah not only healed me, but became a huge source of prevailing comfort for me.

The 99 attributes of Allah validate His **power**, **mercy**, **knowledge**, and **justice**.

"And to Allah belong the best names, so invoke Him by them." Qur'aan, Surah Al A'raf {7:180}

I hope you all benefit from this book in some shape or form, and I pray you all wake up for tahajjud one day…in sha Allah ya Rabbi.

I will make du'aa for each and every single one of you, and all I ask for in return, is the same.

May Allah accept all of our du'aas. The ones we have made in the past, make presently, and yet to make in the future.

Aameen,

Please remember,

"If Allah didn't want to accept your du'aa, He would not have guided you to make it." [Imam Ibn Al Qayyim]

Your sister,

Saba

About the Author

Saba was born and bred in London, UK. She has always had a passion for writing fiction, non-fiction, and poetry ever since she was a little girl. Through her healing journey witnessed and supported by many of her TikTok followers, she decided to document both her experiences and advice in a tell-all self-help book. Saba has made it her mission to help others on their spiritual journey. Saba likes to now call herself a 'tahajjud advocate' due to her successes through this special prayer.

Printed in Great Britain
by Amazon